Grimspound
and
Hound Tor

TWO DESERTED SETTLEMENTS
IN THE
WIDECOMBE AREA

by

Lesley Chapman BA. (Hons.) Exon.

First published in Great Britain in 1996

ORCHARD PUBLICATIONS
2 Orchard Close, Chudleigh, Newton Abbot, Devon TQ13 0LR
Telephone: (01626) 852714

ISBN 1 898964 23 8

Designed, Typeset and Printed for Orchard Publications by
Swift Print
2 High Street
Dawlish
Devon EX7 9HP

CONTENTS

MAP OF THE WIDECOMBE AREA
Showing Grimspound and Hound Tor

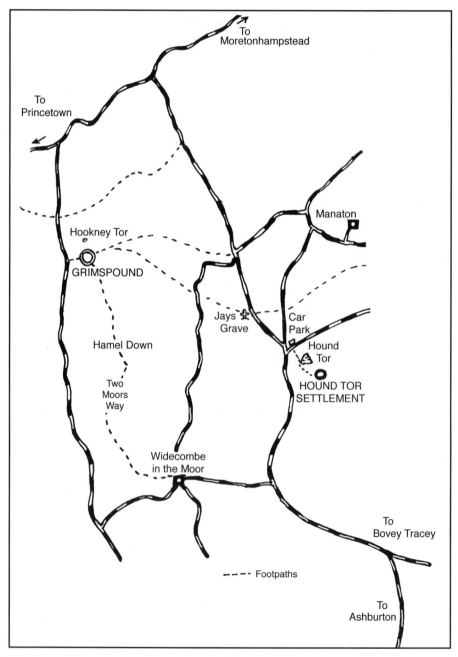

INTRODUCTION

Most people visiting Dartmoor today are impressed by the great natural beauty of the place and consider it to be one of the few remaining places in Britain untouched by man. The history of the moor is however, one of man versus nature. There is abundant evidence of prehistoric man having lived there, for there are large stone monuments scattered all over Dartmoor. There are, too, the occasional old mine workings, testimony to the presence of medieval tin miners, and if one looks carefully enough, there may also be found the remains of quarries, worked during and after the Victorian period. In actual fact, it is man who is largely responsible for the conditions found on the moor today. It is to a great extent a man-made environment. Modern man, we know, is very good at destroying the natural world, but there have been instances in the past when prehistoric man affected his surroundings to such a great extent that they have never recovered.

If a visitor thinks at all about the prehistoric and medieval peoples who lived and worked on the moor, he considers what a harsh life they must have had. The moor was, at various times in its history, a much more inviting place to live than it is today, as there have been changes in the climatic conditions in the past.

During these warm periods, man was able to farm higher on the moor than today, and in greater numbers. It is within these warm spells that man has changed the face of Dartmoor. When the climate deteriorated, the damage done by man to the soil was accelerated by the colder, wetter weather conditions that prevailed, and turned much of the land into peat bogs.

These peat bogs are made of layers of dead, but not decomposed, vegetation, so it is possible to dig down through the layers to see what was growing many hundreds of years ago. Pollen grains survive particularly well, and each species of plant has different shaped pollen. By counting the relative numbers of each species found in a layer of peat we can get a good picture of what Dartmoor was like in the past and how man fits into this scenario.

EARLY MAN ON THE MOOR

The first people to live permanently in Britain were hunters and gatherers. They were, as far as we can tell, nomadic, and moved from inland summer homes to places on the seashore where there were shellfish and seafood to eat. They had small tools and weapons made from flint and seemed to specialise in using bows and arrows. The period to which they belong has been called *Mesolithic,* which means *Middle Stone Age.*

At this time, from about 9,000 to 5,000 years ago, the moor had trees. It was, like most of the rest of England, largely forested with oak, birch, and alders or willows near to rivers or streams. On the highest parts of the moor there would have been open ground, where it is too windy for trees to grow. The forest was not dense, because the soil and height of Dartmoor could not have supported very large trees. It was therefore a very good place to hunt game, fish in the rivers and collect berries, nuts and acorns. In the winter, when food was short, they would have moved down the rivers, either to lower ground or to the seashore to collect shellfish.

Because these people used wood, leather, skins and other materials which soon decay, we very seldom find any trace of where they lived apart from some small flints with which they would have made their arrows and other small tools. They were the first people to start chopping down the trees on Dartmoor to build their houses, boats, tools and weapons. They would have started fires, which would have destroyed trees, making clearings in the forest, or enlarging the areas of the high moor that were without trees.

Around 5,000 years ago farming started in this country. It seems to have spread through Europe from the Middle East. It seemed that it was a good thing to do, for it gave people a permanent home and a more reliable source of food. The first farmers on Dartmoor would have used the open spaces on the high moor and the clearings in the forest to make their fields and build their homes. We can detect what they were doing because the amount of pollen from trees declines suddenly in the peat layers and we start seeing cereal pollen instead. The landscape of Dartmoor was changing rapidly. These farmers left little evidence of their homes on the moor, but it was during this time, called the *Neolithic* or *New Stone Age* that the first stone monuments were built on the moor. Indeed they built monuments all over Britain and Europe, particularly stone tombs for their dead. The farmers had discovered how to make pottery and among their tools are stone axes, essential for chopping down trees. They needed wood for their homes, for tools, ploughs, handles for their axes and for fences to keep their cattle and other animals off their cereal fields. They would have also used wood, for their fires, so the trees rapidly disappeared. Once the trees had gone, the poor soil was exposed to the weather, and blanket bog or peat, started growing high on the moor.

As time went on, they started to build the stone rows and circles for which Dartmoor is well known. Their pottery became better made and highly decorated, and they developed a distinctive style of pot, which we call a Beaker. It was about this time they discovered how to use metals, probably by panning tin and copper from the many streams on Dartmoor. They also discovered gold, and many fine gold ornaments have been found in their burial mounds, or barrows, where they buried their dead with jewellery and tools.

The climate at this time was very warm, so there were quite a few people living on the moor. They were there not only to farm, but also find the gold, tin and copper which they soon learned to make into tools and weapons. They made axe heads from bronze, a mixture of tin and copper, and this invention led us to describe the period as the *Bronze Age,* which began about 4,000 years ago.

These *Bronze Age* people divided the moor into large areas, or estates, by building a system of walls across the moor, called *reaves.* These were only recently recognised as territorial boundaries, and their discovery has given us a much better understanding of the organisation of their society. There is still a lot of work to be done, but it seems that they ensured that everyone had access both to the high pastures and grazing on the moor and to the lower ground around the moor where they could obtain wood, clay for their pots and flints for their tools. Wood was by this time becoming very scarce on the moor, and the peat bogs were growing larger.

GRIMSPOUND

It was at this period in time that Grimspound was built, during the *Middle Bronze Age*. It is one of the best known prehistoric structures on the moor, and easily visited by road. It lies just off the Widecombe to Moretonhampstead road, about 4 miles from Widecombe. There is a small lay-by for parking, and from there you can see the old tin workings in the valley below. Grimspound is not clearly visible from the road, but there is a small track opposite the lay-by on the other side of the road that clearly marks the way.

This track follows the course of the Grims Lake, a small stream that runs through part of the walled enclosure. Approaching from this angle does tend to mislead people, as they come across a breach in the compound wall that looks like the main entrance. It is, in fact a later opening, fashioned when the road from Manaton to Headland Warren was made, which runs right through Grimspound. My advice to visitors is to walk up the path from the road and bear left, climbing the slope to the top of Hookney (Hookner) Tor. From there you will have a wonderful view of Grimspound, and the original main entrance on the far side of the enclosure.

The large enclosure wall is almost circular and within the wall can be seen the remains of hut circles. There are a total of 24, some grouped round the main entrance and the others scattered in the centre. There can also be seen some traces of walls around the opening where the road runs through it, along the lowest side of the boundary circle.

It is obvious from the position of the site in the 'saddle' between two tors and the limited visibility that it has from there, that it is not a site built for defensive purposes. We can therefore assume that the wall was built to keep animals, not people, out (or in). Because we know about the medieval and later pounds, for enclosing stray animals, early investigators of the site called it a pound. Grim is an old name for the devil and was often used by the Saxons to describe prehistoric earthworks, which they evidently regarded as 'diabolical'. The Rev Polwhele was the first to officially record its name in 1797.

He decided that Grimspound was the "seat of judicature" for the area of the River Dart, and that "it is probable that the spot was one of

5

A. C. SHILLIBEAR'S 1829 PLAN OF GRIMSPOUND
(The earliest known plan)

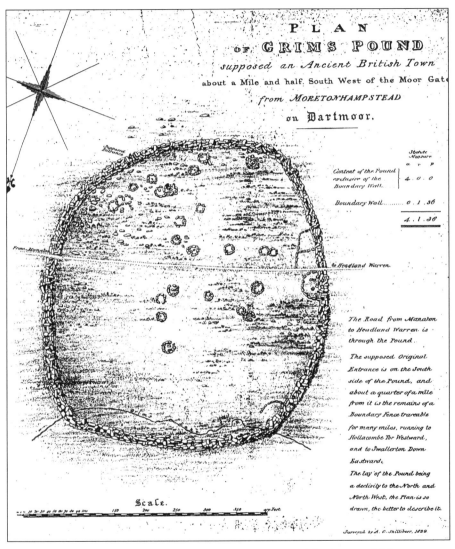

An 1829 survey of Grimspound reproduced courtesy of the Sites and Monuments Office, Exeter. Note Grims Lake running through the bottom of the drawing and the supposed entrance top left of centre.

the principal temples of the Druids". Other antiquarians thought it was a fort of the Iron Age, a summer home for shepherds, a Viking stronghold, a temple of the sun, a pound for herding straying cattle, an encampment for medieval tin miners, a British town of the Roman period, and a Phoenician settlement. It was to settle these debates that the Dartmoor Exploration Committee decided to dig at Grimspound in 1894/96.

There are two plans of the site which date from before the dig. The earliest was drawn by N. Whitely. This shows some huts lying outside the enclosure, which have not been seen or recorded elsewhere,

The walked enclosure of Grimspound, looking down from Hookney Tor.

and could be worth investigation. These old plans are valuable because the 1894/96 excavation not only dug the huts, but also rebuilt at least one of them, Hut 3, which they then enclosed with an iron railing to protect it from cattle. This railing has long since disappeared and the hut now looks much as the others in the enclosure. They also raised the lintels over the doors of the huts, because they did not want them in the way when they excavated. They satisfied themselves also as to the dimensions of the doors in doing so. They also reported that they repaired or rebuilt part of the enclosure wall. It is therefore good to have plans of the original site, and not one that has been altered by Victorian archaeologists.

There were some members of the Committee who disapproved of the rebuilding, and also disagreed with some of the conclusions drawn about the excavation. One subject of the disagreement was about the large round stones found in some of the huts. The committee decided they were placed at the top of the thatch of the roof, to hold the apex together. Mr R. Hansford Worth, in his book "Dartmoor" says this was ridiculous, as it conjured up a picture of these people sitting in their huts with these stones perched on the roof like "the sword of Damocles", or else asphyxiating as the roof would have had no hole for the smoke from the fire to escape!

THE ENCLOSURE WALL

According to the excavation by Rev Sabine Baring-Gould in 1894/96, the entrance was paved with three steps down into the compound. Today it is possible to see the paving, but more difficult to pick up the steps. The wall on the left of the entrance was built in different manner to the wall on the right. This also is difficult to discern, but is interesting because of the recent excavations of Shaugh Moor and Holne Moor, where it was shown that walls were built by teams or gangs, each working over a length of about 10 yards. This was evident from the building styles of the wall. A friend suggested that some parts were built by men, while the women, assisted perhaps by children, built the other. It may well be, but could equally be just a difference in style or technique.

Similar differences in style can be made out in the Grimspound wall, where there are some sections made of small stones, less than 2 feet in length, and other parts where very large stones, over 3 feet have been used. This may mean nothing because we know that the excavators of Grimspound at the end of the last century rebuilt some of the wall, and it could be their handiwork we are looking at.

The wall itself was thought by the committee to be made up of two concentric rings, both about 3 feet thick, and with a gap in the middle, also about 3 feet wide. There is no evidence that the

The right hand wall of Grimspound entrance showing various sizes of the granite blocks used.

Grimspound hut circle.

9

The wall of Grimspound, showing areas of large and small stones used in the building.

The entrance to Grimspound with Hookney (Hookner) Tor in the background.

10

NICHOLAS WITLEY'S 1855 PLAN OF GRIMSPOUND

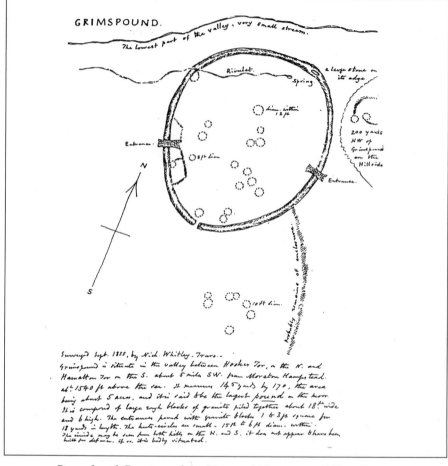

Reproduced Courtesy of the Sites and Monuments Office, Exeter.
The text reads …
Surveyed Sept. 1855, by Nick Whitley, Truro. Grimspound is situate in the valley
between Hookner Tor, on the N. and Hamelton Tor on the S. about 5 miles SW. from
Moreton Hampstead. abt 1540 ft above the sea. It measures 145 yards by 170, the
area being about 5 acres, and it is said to be the largest pound on the moor. It is
composed of large rough blocks of granite piled together 18 ft wide and 6 high. The
entrances paved with granite blocks 1 to 3 ft square for 18 yards in length. The hut -
circles are small - 15 ft to 6 ft diam, within. The inside may be seen from both hills
on the N. and S. it does not appear to have been built for defence, if so, it's badly
situated.

11

Committee were right, and it is more likely that the wall was a solid one, about 9 feet wide but only 4 to 5 feet high. We expect that cattle were kept in the compound, as evidence of them has been found by modern excavation at other sites, like Shaugh Moor on Southern Dartmoor, where their hoof prints have been found, in mud that lay undisturbed for 4,000 years.

The external wall would therefore be needed to keep the cattle safe at night, although I suspect that a determined wolf (who lived here in those days) could have climbed over the wall easily, so perhaps there was a fence or hedge built along the top. It is certainly not a defensive structure, as the site of Grimspound is not in a suitable position, any determined enemy could spring a surprise attack virtually unseen.

Artist's reconstruction of Grimspound Hut

THE HUTS OF GRIMSPOUND

The excavation of 1894/96 identified 24 huts inside the wall of Grimspound, and some of these were dug up. Although the excavation was not as careful as a modern one would be, they do report that they left stones alone that were embedded in the soil, only moving those that were lying loose. They dug the soil out of the huts until they could see what they described as the floor, made out of stonier, gravely soil than the peat or *meat earth* that overlay it.

They found that some of the huts did not have any signs of habitation and concluded that these were used for stores or to keep animals. The huts near the entrance, except hut number 12, all appear to have been used for stores or shelter for stock. Number 2 at the far side of the settlement also had no signs of household quarters, and was probably also a store hut. Huts 22, 23 and 24 are not mentioned in their report but are shown on their plan.

The huts are all circular and have an entrance or doorway defined by lintels and jamb stones. The entrances were paved with naturally flat stones. Some of the huts that were occupied had a porch to protect the doorway from the weather, but it also served to keep animals out. Most of these porches are curved and can still be made out today, especially at hut 3. The entrances all face away from the north-westerly winds, like other huts of other settlements of the date, such as Dean Moor on the southern edge of Dartmoor.

The diameter of the inside of the huts ranges from 9feet to about 15 feet (3 to 4.5m) but the walls, made of slabs set upright in the ground, with the spaces between them filled with smaller stones, were about 2 or 3 feet (0.6m-1m) thick. It seems likely that the walls were then packed with peat to fill in the smaller gaps and make them draught-proof. The 1894/96 excavation did not have the knowledge to look for post-holes, distinctive marks left in the soil where wooden posts once stood, but at other places, such as Holne Moor, modern excavations have shown that similar huts there were lined with wooden planks. This would have made them just as cosy as a modern dwelling, although they were very small by our standards.

PLAN OF GRIMSPOUND FOR THE 1894/96 EXCAVATION
drawn from R. Hansford Worth's originals

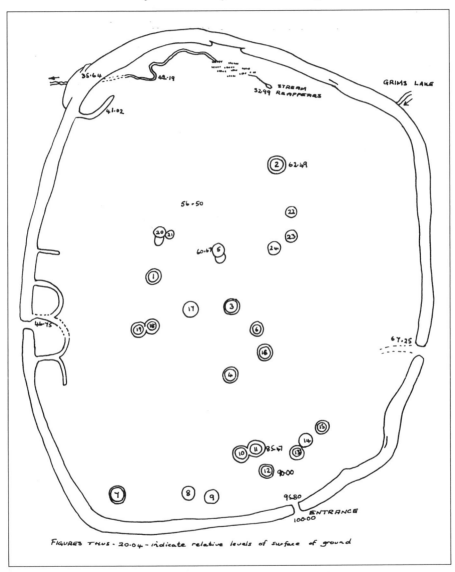

NOTE. *All the hut numbers given in this book use these numbers.*

R. HANSFORD WORTH'S HUT PLANS

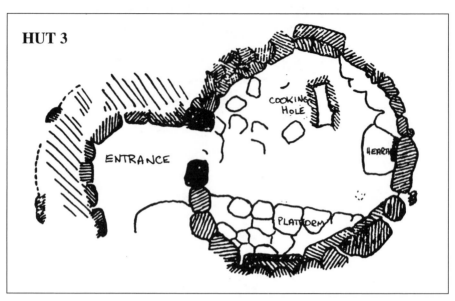

HUT 3

COOKING HOLE

ENTRANCE

HEARTH

PLATFORM

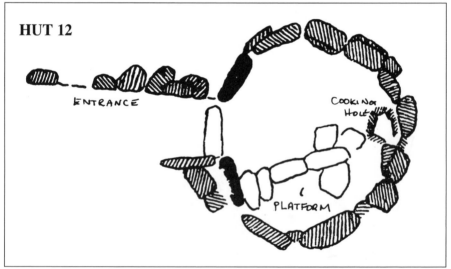

HUT 12

ENTRANCE

COOKING HOLE

PLATFORM

0   5   10   16

FEET.

INSIDE THE HUTS

The Rev Sabine Baring-Gould and the other members of the Dartmoor Exploration Committee, who dug at Grimspound, identified those huts that were occupied by the presence of a hearth. These were found to be either opposite the door or in the centre of the hut. The ash in the hearths was carefully examined, and found to contain the ash from oak and willow trees, all of them very small twigs, no large logs. There was also peat ash, which shows that there were very few trees left on the moor by this time, and that the peat bogs had grown large enough for them to be cut for fuel. Peat in quantity could well have been used for building, as well as for fuel.

Close to the hearths they found some holes, which they decided were cooking pits. As the pottery of the time was not fire-proof, they used to heat water and food by placing a pot in a pit and filling it with water. Stones heated in the fire were then dropped into the water. There have been plenty of these fire-marked stones found on other sites, but very few at Grimspound. One explanation could be that very few of the pebbles normally used for this purpose were available in the area, and they used ordinary stones of granite instead. These would have shattered after being heated and dropped into cold water. This method of cooking has been proved correct by modern excavations at other places on the moor and elsewhere.

It is interesting to speculate on what they would have eaten, and how they would have cooked it. They had some domesticated animals, notably cattle and sheep, so had milk (from both), butter, cheese and meat. They would have collected eggs from the wild birds, especially the water-fowl on the moor, so I expect omelettes were on the menu. Stews would have been easy to prepare using wild plants, beans, roots and cereals, as well as meat. Bread, baked from the cereals, would have looked very different from our own but would have been filling, and quite tasty with fresh butter and cheese. Porridge, perhaps sweetened with honey or fruit, would have warmed them up on cold mornings, and for fun, they probably heated corn and made pop-corn. Wild game would have included deer, hare and wild boar, as well as any of the many birds, like pigeons and duck.

They would not have had potatoes, rabbits, carrots or many other foods which have been introduced by the Romans, the Normans, or brought back from the New World.

One other feature of the interior of the huts was what the Committee called a 'dias'; a raised area of stones found, as a rule to the right of the hut entrance. This would have been where they made their bed, the raised floor giving them protection from damp. Their beds were probably made from straw, but heather or bracken will also make a nice soft mattress. They had woven blankets, but when the weather was very cold, could also have used sheepskin, or the furry skins of wild animals, like bears or wolves which lived here in those days.

Their clothing would have been made from the same materials, sewn together using bone needles. The "Ice Man," recently found in the Alps, dates from much the same time as Grimspound and was dressed in trousers and jacket made from skin, and had shoes that were sewn to fit his feet. Fine weapons and personal ornaments are found in their graves. A dagger was found in a barrow on the tor overlooking Grimspound. They were also fond of jewellery, especially gold, though they may have kept this for 'best' or for their religious ceremonies. There is also a chance they made the jewellery solely for burying with their dead, but some of it is so beautiful, I doubt if they could have resisted wearing it when they were alive!

Apart from bone, which they used for sewing needles and their small tools, they also used leather, wood and fibre for making tools, weapons, clothing and other implements. On Dartmoor all these organic materials have perished in the acidic soil and peat so all we have are the stone and flint, or occasional piece of pottery.

When Grimspound was excavated very few small finds were made. They found very little pottery, and no flint at all. Some time later, however, a gentleman visiting the site found a flint, after it had been washed out of the soil following heavy rain. This flint is an arrowhead, and is beautifully fashioned. Its form goes beyond the purely functional, and is designed as a work of art, with care and attention. These 'barbed and tanged' arrowheads are typical of the *Bronze Age* and are very difficult to make. It appears that these people were highly skilled in using and shaping flint.

As wood decays, it leaves traces in the ground which modern archaeologists can identify. These post-hole features have been found at other sites on the moor and have shown that, besides the stone huts, there were many buildings, and features of the stone buildings that have long since disappeared. It is highly likely that within the huts and within the compound, there were many features and buildings made from wood. At Shaugh Moor it was shown that before the stone buildings were made, there was an earlier phase, made from wood. It suggests that people moved into the area and built easily erected huts, possibly from wood they brought with them, and after a while, deciding that they liked living there, built the more permanent stone buildings.

We do not know if this was the case at Grimspound, as the Victorian excavators did not know how to recognise post-holes, and it is not likely that the site will be dug by modern methods. Modern archaeology is so expensive that only sites that are threatened by building roads, or re-development, etc. are dug. Unless someone decides to build a motorway through Grimspound, it is safe.

It is certain, however, that within the compound and within the huts, there were many articles made from wood. There may have been a fence round the huts to stop the cattle getting too close; there may have been small areas fenced off to create gardens to grow beans and herbs; there may have been other huts, built from wood, used to keep chickens or geese and there would have been frames or racks for the drying of skins or hanging meat out to cure. When a visitor goes to Grimspound, he is seeing just a very small part of what was once there, and has to close his eyes, use his imagination and try to recreate the whole living scene in the mind.

The most important things that are missing are the roofs of the huts. These would have been constructed from wooden rafters, probably covered with some kind of thatch. This could have been made from straw or heather, and was probably held up with purloins and tied in place with thongs. This would have been quite waterproof, as are thatched houses today. An alternative is that the roofs were

18

Grimspound. Huts 20 and 21 as they are today.

Grimspound. \Hut 1 as it is today.

covered with peat, as were the 'black houses' of Scotland until modern times. Some of the settlements of this period have evidence of both arable (cereal) farming and of pastoral (animal husbandry). Others have only one or other of these, and judging from the absence of fields suitable for crops in the vicinity of Grimspound, it is thought that Grimspound concentrated on the farming of animals, probably chiefly cattle, but possibly also sheep. They would have exchanged these for the things they did not have, but needed, such as cereals, flint, pottery and timber.

There were no quern stones (which are used to grind corn) found at Grimspound, which suggests they bought their cereal already ground from an arable farming settlement. Flint is not natural to Dartmoor, and would have had to come from either the coast, where flint pebbles can be found, or from flint mines in chalky areas, in South East Devon. The Committee decided that the Grimspound pottery was not made from the natural china clay that is found on the moor, so had to come from outside the region. Timber, as we have seen, was getting scarce on the moor, and it is likely that no large trees remained, so any large pieces would have had to have been brought in from lowland areas.

There was no sign of any metal to be seen at Grimspound, so the Committee decided the settlement dated from the *Neolithic* period, before the discovery of metal-working. We are now sure that Grimspound belongs, like the other stone hut enclosures, to the *Bronze Age*. The absence of any copper can be accounted for by many theories.

Firstly, the 1894/96 excavation was not complete; only some of the huts were dug (and those were done very quickly) and some small quantities of metal could easily have been missed. Secondly, they may not have been involved with the mining and smelting of the tin and copper, making bronze, but have bought the finished product from the group who were producing it. Thirdly, they may have taken their time when they came to leave and abandon the site, clearing up very carefully behind them, especially taking the valuable metal objects with them.

At other places on the moor, there is evidence of prehistoric copper working, where the moulds for making bronze axe-heads have been found.

Towards the end of the *Bronze Age* there was a definite change in the climatic conditions. There was more rain, and the temperature became much colder. The increase in water falling on the moor speeded up the growth of the peat bog areas, and the fall in temperature meant that cereal crops could not be grown at such high altitudes. One by one the settlements must have been abandoned, as people living there faced the choice of moving to lower ground or starving. There are signs that all over England *Bronze Age* people tried to propitiate their gods by making offerings to them. In rivers, streams, ponds and lakes we have found weapons and other fine objects, like shields, which seem to have been thrown there to try to get the water gods to stop the rain. The *Bronze Age* gods refused to listen and conditions got worse all over the country. It was on the marginal lands, like Dartmoor, that the effects were most severely felt, as it drove people to abandon their homes, where they had lived for centuries.

As these people left, the land which because it had been heavily grazed and was good pasture, became less nutritious, and inedible plants, like bracken spread. There may have still been some summer grazing available for the people who drove their cattle and sheep onto the moors, but they then had to either find permanent shelter for them back on the lowlands, or to cull most of the herd in the autumn.

Dartmoor was used during the following period, the *Iron Age,* as some places like Kes Tor date from that time. For the most part though, the moor was left to itself in the winter, and only in summer were there domesticated animals on the moor. Wild animals would have found it a very good place, especially those that were afraid of man. Hunting parties during the *Iron Age* and the Roman period would have found plenty of deer, for example, to provide venison for a change of diet.

There may have been some intrepid miners on the moors, finding tin, copper and silver. Pewter was particularly popular during the Roman period, so it is highly likely that they were there looking for the tin and lead to make pewter. By the time the Romans left this country, about 500AD. the weather was starting to turn warmer, and men once again began to look to the moor for a place to live.

THE EARLY FOUNDATIONS OF HOUND TOR

Just off the road from Widecombe to Manaton lies Hound Tor. There is a large car park on the right (usually with an ice cream van) and the paths to the tor are clearly visible. The area is a favourite for ponies and small herds can usually be seen as you walk up the slope to the tor. Keep to the right of the tor and follow the track down the other side. As you proceed down the hill, the outline of ancient fields can be seen and if you look carefully, you will notice there are lines in the fields, which are the marks left behind from ploughing.

As you walk farther down, you will also notice you are entering a field, bordered by a stone wall. At about this point, the ruined huts of the settlement of Hound Tor will become visible. There are 11 buildings, 8 of them are houses and 3 are barns used for drying and storing corn. The site was excavated between 1961 to 1975 by Mrs E. Marie Winter, and was written up and published after she had died, by Guy Beresford. The excavation was much more careful than the 1894/96 dig at Grimspound, so we have more details about this site.

This village lies on the very margin of the present tree line on this side of the moor. The valley below is today a wood, and the many bluebells (a stunted variety) amongst the bracken around the slope of Hound Tor suggest the trees once grew much higher than today, as bluebells are a woodland species.

There was a long sequence of buildings, all superimposed. The oldest appears to have been a settlement belonging to the same date as Grimspound, that is, the *Middle Bronze Age,* about 1,000 bc. The site was abandoned about 500 bc when the weather deteriorated. As the climate improved, about a thousand years later, 500 ad. the site was attractive for early Saxon age farmers. The stones had been cleared during the prehistoric phase, and the position is sheltered from the prevailing winds by the slope of Hound Tor, which is why the *Bronze Age* settlers had found it attractive.

The Saxon Age houses were built from wood and turf, with wattles inside the walls, perhaps covered in mud or plaster. They were probably thatched but could have had their roofs made from turf, which is quite waterproof and durable, as used by people in Scotland and

22

PLAN OF HOUND TOR VILLAGE
Drawn from G Beresford's Plan

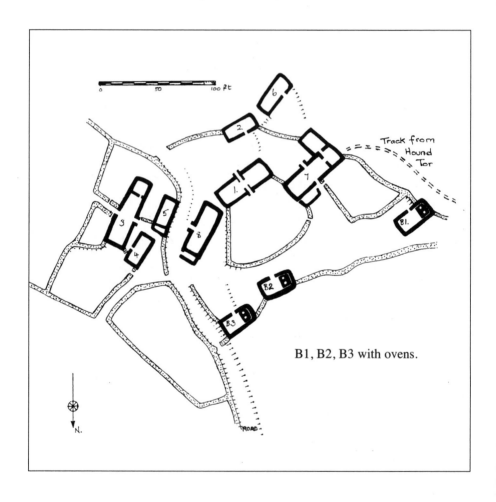

Track from
Hound
Tor

B1, B2, B3 with ovens.

N.

Ireland until modern times. The builders of these houses may have been native Celtic peoples, not Saxon newcomers, as the shapes of the fields of the settlements are rounded, which is evocative of field shapes found in the Celtic areas of Britain, especially Cornwall. The houses though, are typical of Early Saxon buildings.

These turf houses were only identified from the post-holes in the ground and the living floor areas these post-holes enclosed. The excavation removed the top-soil, down to a level of gravel, called *growan,* which is light in colour. The decayed remains of wooden posts, are very dark and therefore show up clearly in the light growan. The earliest of the huts were of a type that suggests they were for summer occupation only, used perhaps by herdsmen who stayed on the moors until the calves were tender, as was the case in historical times. Later the houses become more substantial and suitable for year-long occupation, as the climate got warmer and warmer.

The number and layout of the post-holes suggest that the turf houses were rebuilt every 30 or so years, possibly by each succeeding generation. Eventually between 1250 and 1350 ad. these turf houses were replaced by stone buildings, which have left the remains that are visible today.

These are, like the turf houses, long structures, basically divided into two rooms, with doors in the long walls, which were between 2 and 3 feet thick, and between 6 and 7 feet high. The houses ranged in size from 57 feet long and 14 feet wide (house 3) to 23 feet by 10 feet (house 2). They were built from undressed stones collected from the moor, and packed with soil or *growan* to fill in the spaces. The doors were hung on large wooden posts and were made of wood. Because of the acidity of the soil, it was not possible to see whether they had metal locks and keys, as found elsewhere in the country, or wooden door furniture. The thresholds of the doors were paved with flat stones. The roof of the house would have been thatched either with straw, heather or rushes.

The lower half of the house, called the byre, was where cattle would have been kept during the winter. The byre had a drain which can still be clearly seen in the houses. Excavation showed that the cattle were tethered with their heads facing the walls, so that their excrement fell into the area of the drain. Areas which housed their feed mangers have also been uncovered. People have often shared their homes with farm animals as it keeps the creatures safe and warm, and also helps keep the human occupants warm.

The higher end of the house had a central hearth, defined by hearth stones, and some had wattle and daub chimney hoods. There were some cooking pits near to the hearths; these were used in the way described in the chapter on Grimspound. Some of the houses were found to be too cramped and other rooms were built on. House 7 for example, had a *pentice* or out-house and another smaller living room plus another inner room.

Around the houses were gardens, where they would have grown vegetables, mostly beans and peas which were the staple diet before the introduction of potatoes in Elizabethan times. They may also have grown herbs, both for flavouring food and also as medical remedies. By the 13th Century rabbits were established in this country and were kept on warrens. There were many warrens on the moor, and rabbit made a welcome addition to the menu. Rabbits were deliberately introduced in this period to provide fresh winter meat, as most of the cattle were killed in the autumn and salted.

There was not much rubbish left behind when the settlers moved out, which is a pity from the archaeological point of view, for there were few artefacts to give precise dates to the buildings. There was one coin, which dates to the period 1253-60, the reign of Henry III, and some shards of pottery that were originally made at Crockerton, in Dorset.

The fields surrounding the settlement show the marks of ploughing, so we know they were growing cereals and storing them in the corn-drying barns that lie to the north of the settlement. These were identified partly because there was not the usual hearth and living area associated with houses, but also because they only had one entrance. They also had ovens, which would have been kept warm to keep the corn dry, which can be clearly seen today. These barns belong to the last phase of building and occupation of the site in the early 14th Century. It was about this time that two disasters occurred, with

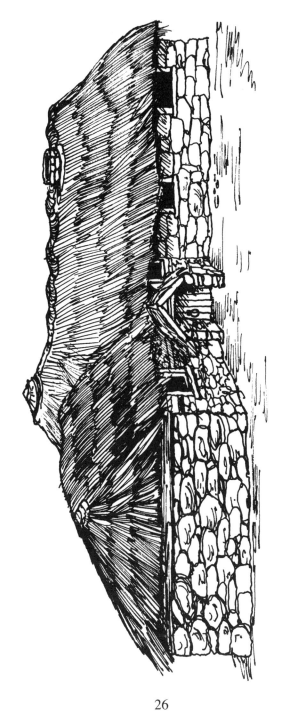

Artist's reconstruction of house number 7, Hound Tor.

failing, and eventually failed harvests. The first was that the climate deteriorated once again, and farmers were faced with starvation. The farmers on marginal lands, such as at Hound Tor, were forced to the brink of survival. Some of these farmers would have given up and moved, others would have stayed on, hoping for a change of fortune.

Then the Black Death swept across the country. This plague killed about a third of all Europeans, and changed the ways of lives of many people in Europe for ever. It struck England in 1348, and is recorded as having come at a time following 40 days and nights of rain, a deluge which started on St Swithins Day. This led to the old saying:

"St Swithins Day, If thou dost rain,
For forty days, it will remain.
St Swithins Day, if thou be fair,
For 40 days 'twill rain na mair."

The plague and the weather would have forced the remaining farmers off their lands, those who survived the plague, that is. Because it killed so many, there must have been farms around, on better lands which were now unoccupied. So a combination of catastrophes led to the abandonment of Hound Tor village.

There are other medieval deserted settlements on the moor, as well as many prehistoric remains of homes, all witness to the changing weather conditions this country has undergone, and, to some extent, the exploitation of a fragile landscape by man.

Dartmoor is now a protected area, a National Park, which will save it from further exploitation by man. We do have some effect there, even today. Overhead photographs of the site of Grimspound taken some years apart show the damage people visiting the site cause, just by walking on it. We need to preserve these monuments on Dartmoor as best we can, because it is from here with its environmental evidence, that we can build a fuller picture of man's life in the past. We can see how important the weather was, how fragile soils can be destroyed, how important forests and trees were, and hopefully we can learn from our past mistakes.

Hound Tor. House number 7 as it is today - the living area.

The lower half of house number 7 as it is today showing drain for the animals.

BIBLIOGRAPHY

S BARING GOULD "First Report of the Dartmoor Exploration Committee: The Exploration of Grimspound" *Transactions of the Devonshire Association* No 26 (1894) pp 101-121

G BERESFORD "Three Deserted Medieval Settlements on Dartmoor: A Report on the late E Marie Minter's Excavations" *Medieval Archaeology* No 23 pp 98-158

A FLEMING "The Dartmoor Reave Project" *Current Archaeology* pp 234-237

A FLEMING "Dartmoor Reaves" *Devon Archaeology* No 3 (1985) pp 1-13

A FOX "South West England" (1973 Revised ed) p 103

J GOVER, A MAWER & F STENTON "The Place Names of Devon" (1931) p482

R HANSFORD WORTH "Dartmoor" 1953

R POLWHELE "History of Devon" Vol 1 (1797) p151

S R ROWE "A Perambulation of the Ancient (sic) and Royal Forest of Dartmoor" (3rd Edition) 1896

I G SIMMONS "Environment and Early Man on Dartmoor" *Proceedings of the Prehistoric Society* No 35 (1969) pp 203-215

Photographs were taken by the author, who wishes to thank the staff of the Sites and Monuments Office, Exeter, and the Technicians of the Archaeology Dept, Exeter University for their help in producing this book. I would also like to thank Kate Lowe for her help in compiling the material within.